YOU CHOOSE

DANGEROUS RESCUE FROM AMIENS PRISON

INTERACTIVE WORLD WAR II MISSIONS

by Matt Doeden

CAPSTONE PRESS
a capstone imprint

Published by Capstone Press, an imprint of Capstone
1710 Roe Crest Drive, North Mankato, Minnesota 56003
capstonepub.com

Library of Congress Cataloging-in-Publication Data
is available on the Library of Congress website.

ISBN: 9798875244575 (hardcover)
ISBN: 9798875244544 (paperback)
ISBN: 9798875244551 (ebook PDF)

Summary: Midway through World War II, many French Resistance members were being held prisoner at Amiens Prison in German-occupied France. On February 18, 1944, the Allies conducted Operation Jericho, a daring rescue mission to set them free. Would you rather be an Allied pilot who bombs holes in the prison walls or a free French Resistance fighter who helps whisk escaping prisoners to freedom? Now is your chance to do both—and more! In this interactive adventure, YOU CHOOSE the paths that will lead you and others to freedom . . . or spell your doom!

Editorial Credits
Designer: Bobbie Nuytten; Media Researcher: Svetlana Zhurkin;
Production Specialist: Katy LaVigne

Image Credits
Alamy: Maurice Savage, 43, Robert Boulware, 16; Associated Press: 4; Bridgeman Images: © Look and Learn, cover (bottom), 22, 87, Tallandier, 18, 52, 60; Dreamstime: Kevin M. Mccarthy, 108 (top); Getty Images: Hulton Archive/Fox Photos, 108 (bottom), Hulton Archive/FPG, 37, Hulton Archive/Keystone, 10, 31, 101, Hulton Archive/Picture Post/Haywood Magee, 105, Martial Colomb, 97; Mary Evans: Raymond Sheppard Collection, 47; Shutterstock: Buch and Bee (airplane emblem), 5 and throughout, Dirk M. de Boer, 69, jollys_art (old paper), cover and throughout, Keith Tarrier, 8, 12, 40, 72, 98, Kzenon, 67, Olemac, 81, Pablo Caridad (paper file), 1 and throughout, Peter Hermes Furian, 6–7, Valentin Agapov (folder), back cover and throughout, Vladimir Mulder, 64, Yurchenko S, 34; SuperStock: PL Photography Limited/Piemags, cover (top), Sydney Morning Herald/Department of Air, 103

Printed and bound in China. 6461

TABLE OF CONTENTS

Damaged Amiens Prison is seen through the huge breach in the outer wall as a result of an air raid.

ABOUT YOUR ADVENTURE

YOU are living in Europe during World War II (1939–1945), and your life is about to take a dramatic turn. In northern France stands Amiens Prison, where the Nazis hold French Resistance fighters and Allied soldiers captive. You might be an Allied bomber pilot or French Resistance member taking part in a daring mission to set the prisoners free. Or you might be a prisoner at Amiens trying to escape during Operation Jericho.

Whichever fate you face, YOU CHOOSE the paths that will determine your destiny. If you choose wisely, you and others may finally find a way to freedom. But one wrong choice could also lead to total failure. Will your decisions help you succeed or spell your doom?

Turn the page to begin your adventure.

AMIENS PRISON AND OPERATION JERICHO

The Prison

Amiens Prison was located just outside the town of Amiens in the northern part of German-occupied France. The prison grounds consisted primarily of a tall, T-shaped prison building and a couple of prison guard barracks surrounded by a high stone wall. By early 1944, hundreds of Allied prisoners of war, including important members of the French Resistance, were being held there.

Key Words

Allies—a group of countries including the United States, Great Britain, the Soviet Union, China, and France that fought together in World War II

Axis powers—a group of countries including Germany, Italy, and Japan that fought together in World War II

French Resistance—French citizens who secretly fought against the Nazis occupying France during World War II

Nazi—a member of a political party led by Adolf Hitler; the Nazis ruled Germany from 1933 to 1945

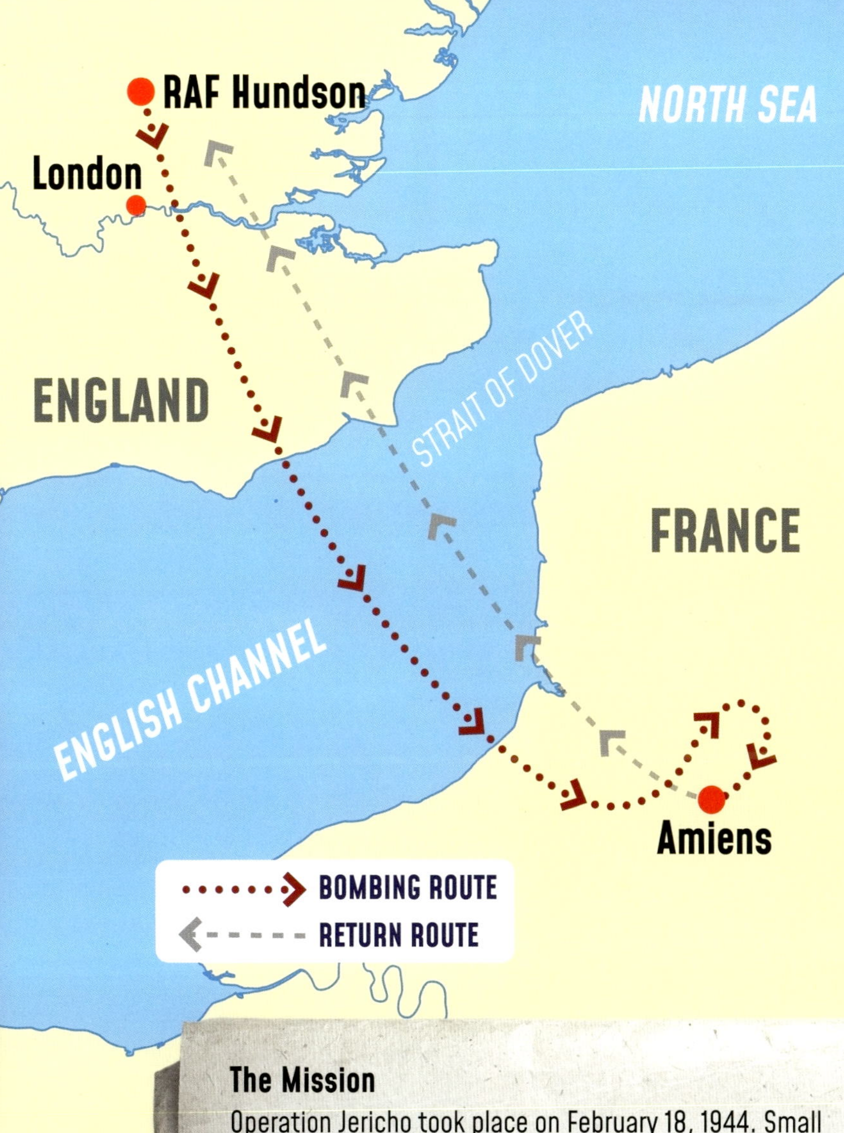

The Mission

Operation Jericho took place on February 18, 1944. Small Allied bombers took off from England and flew into northern France. The bombers targeted Amiens Prison near the town of Amiens, France. The bombers blew holes in the prison's walls, as well as the main building. More than 200 prisoners escaped, although many were soon recaptured by the German forces.

X100
JET PIPE °C
20
10
30
OIL
P.S.I.
0
40
SLOW
FAST
TYPE KB 301/02
KELVIN

Chapter 1

PRISON FORTRESS

World War II rages across Europe. Nazi Germany has taken control of France, but it has been hindered by groups of French Resistance fighters and spies. These groups have become a key source of military intelligence for the Allies, and the Nazis have gone to great lengths to capture and imprison as many Resistance fighters as they can.

Many fighters—along with other Allied prisoners—are kept at Amiens Prison. Located in northern France, the prison's dark stone walls and buildings stand out on a blanket of white snow. But the conditions inside the prison are rough. Prisoners are starving. The Germans, growing more and more desperate, have begun to execute their captives. It's a desperate time for the men locked up inside.

Unknown to them, activities beyond the prison's walls are about to change everything. Nearby, Resistance fighters gather to help carry out a daring rescue mission. The fighters have their eyes on the skies, knowing a wave of Allied fighter planes could be coming any day.

French Resistance members on the lookout for Allied airplanes dropping supplies to support their fight against the Nazis

Far to the west, plans are underway to have a group of Allied planes take to the skies. The aircraft include small, maneuverable DH.98 Mosquitoes that can fly very low to the ground and larger Hawker Typhoons that will serve as escorts. Their mission will be to make a dangerous flight toward Amiens Prison.

You have been through a lot already in World War II. You've seen more death and destruction than anyone should see. You know the horrors of war. You have no idea what today will bring. But one of the most daring prison rescues of the war is about to happen, and you have a front-row seat.

Are you ready? Can you make it out alive?

To take the controls of a Mosquito bomber plane, turn to page 13.

To be an escaping prisoner, turn to page 41.

To join the French Resistance and support the mission, turn to page 73.

X100
ET PIPE °C
OIL
P.S.I.
SLOW
FAST
TYPE KB 501/02
KELVIN

Chapter 2

AIR RAID

It's February 18, 1944, and you are an Australian bomber pilot based out of Great Britain. You're about to take on one of the most daring missions of your military career, and you feel both excited and nervous.

The hum of your propellers rattles your plane as you grip the control stick of your DH.98 Mosquito. The small plane, made mostly of wood, hangs just a few dozen feet above the choppy waters of the English Channel. This narrow stretch of ocean separates England from northern France.

You're flying so low that your plane leaves a wake on the water below. Low, gray clouds hang over the water. In the mist and sleet, the enemy will never expect an air raid.

Turn the page.

Your radio crackles. "Keep low everyone," says Captain Percy Charles Pickard, the commander of the mission. "The Germans can't know we're coming. Everything depends on this being a surprise. We'll be crossing into France in a few minutes. Stay at treetop level."

You scan the horizon, searching for a hint of land. But driving snow and sleet make it impossible to see anything.

You focus on the task in front of you. The raid mission is split into three groups. You'll take turns bombing the prison. Group one will try to blast through the prison's outer walls.

Group two—your group—will be right behind them. Your job is to bomb the prison buildings themselves. The grounds are made up of a large three-story prison building, formed in the shape of a T, and single-story guards' barracks that stand attached to two of the ends.

Your target is one of the guard barracks. Others will target the prison itself. The plan is for explosives to blow open the cell doors of the prisoners inside. It will require incredible skill. It will also be dangerous for both the pilots and the prisoners.

Finally, you spot land ahead. A blanket of fresh white snow covers the French countryside. As ordered, you stay low, just above the treetops. If you go too high, the Germans' radar will spot you and warn the prison guards of your approach. You can't let that happen. While flying so low is risky, it's not as risky as facing anti-aircraft fire once you arrive.

You're supposed to be in formation with five other planes, but staying together in the snowy weather has been difficult. You can barely make out the Mosquito just ahead of you, so you hold course and follow.

Turn the page.

Two DH.98 Mosquito bombers flying on a mission

As you get farther inland, the snow lets up a bit. Visibility improves, and you're able to get together with the other four planes.

The Mosquito is designed to fly low. The plane is a lightweight bomber that can get in, drop its bomb, and get out in a hurry. But you've never flown like this. You're so close to the ground that you kick up snow behind you, like the wake behind a boat. At one point, you have to pull up quickly to avoid running into a tree.

"Wave one is approaching," calls out Pickard over the radio. "Wave two, you'll be right behind them."

A dark spot on the white snow ahead marks your target—Amiens Prison. Ahead of you, the first wave of planes is dropping their bombs. The pilots actually drop them on the ground, allowing them to skip ahead into their target—the prison's outer walls.

The Nazi guards will react quickly once they realize they're under attack. Should you speed up to get there faster? Or is it better to let the first wave's bombs explode before you approach?

To speed up, turn to page 18.

To hang back, turn to page 20.

Smoke rises from the Amiens Prison buildings hit by Allied bombers.

"Let's go," you mutter to yourself as you pick up speed. The prison grows rapidly in your windshield as you approach. An orange ball of flame erupts on the east side of the outer wall. Then another.

You focus on your target, the corner of the main building. You'll aim for the ground just in front of it, knowing that your bomb is on an eleven-second fuse.

Your Mosquito speeds over the outer wall just as the last bomb from the first wave explodes. Suddenly, your whole plane is engulfed in flames.

You feel the plane bank hard to the left as debris from the explosion slams into one of your wings.

"I'm hit!" you call into the radio.

Your plane rattles and shakes as you fight to keep it in the air. Behind you, the rest of the second wave is dropping bombs. You can hear the explosions as you fight to keep control of your wounded plane.

Turn to page 28.

You're eager to get in and drop your payload. But you know better than to follow too closely. If you do, you could get caught up in an explosion. You've got to wait until the first wave of bombs have all detonated. So, you hang back just a few more seconds.

You watch as the explosions rock the prison's outer walls. Not all of the bombs hit their marks, but enough of them do. The explosions blast through two of the prison's outer walls—exactly as planned. Now your wave just has to hit the large three-story building itself, along with the smaller attached guards' barracks, to give the prisoners an escape. It's a desperate move. You know that bombing the prison, with the prisoners inside, will kill many of the men you're trying to save. But there's no choice. With the Germans executing prisoners, you have to give these men the best shot you can at escape.

You bring your plane in straight toward the corner of the three-story prison building, where the barracks building is attached. One of the other planes in your wave is ahead of you. You watch as the pilot misses his target—the foundation of the large prison building itself. The errant bomb explodes dozens of yards away, doing no damage at all.

You've got just a second or two to make a quick decision. Should you stick with your original target of the guards' barracks? Or would it be better to try to hit the main building to make up for the first pilot's miss?

To aim for your original target, turn to page 22.

To switch targets at the last second, turn to page 30.

It's too risky to switch targets at the last moment. You're more likely to miss everything. So, you lock in on your target—the ground just a few dozen feet in front of the corner of the guards' barracks. You release the bomb and immediately pull up and bank to the left.

German guards panic during the surprise air raid on Amiens Prison.

Behind you, the bomb slams into the ground and skips ahead, like a stone skipping on water. It crashes right into the corner of the building. It detonates, blasting rubble in every direction. Within moments, prisoners are pouring out of the blasted building and rushing for the walls.

"They're out," Pickard says over the radio. You look back and see men coming out of the building. The guards are caught by surprise, but they'll regroup in moments. They'll be shooting—both at the escaping prisoners and at any planes that come too close.

If you're willing to take the risk, you could make another pass to strafe the guard's barracks. Opening fire on the guards might buy the prisoners some time, but it will be dangerous.

To turn around and fire on the barracks, turn to page 24.

To get out safely while you still can, turn to page 38.

You know this will be your only chance to help the escaping prisoners. You came here to break them out, and flying for safety just doesn't feel right.

"I'm making another pass," you say on the radio. "I'm going to strafe the guards' barracks to see if I can buy those POWs a little more time to escape."

You bank your plane hard and swoop back around. You can see that most of the prison's guards are centered around the barracks. You open fire on the building, shooting your guns on their position. You doubt you'll hit much, but you're hoping you can give the prisoners a few more precious seconds to escape.

Pickard's voice comes back over the radio. "Red Daddy," he calls out. It's a code word. Your mission is complete, but German aircraft are coming. Pickard is telling you that it's time to get out, before the German airplanes arrive.

You know that making your escape is going to be tricky. The incoming German fighters will be a bigger danger to you if you climb higher. But if you stay low, you're at risk of getting whacked by anti-aircraft fire. With only seconds to decide, which choice do you make? Do you stay low or climb higher?

To stay low, turn to page 26.

To climb higher, turn to page 31.

Getting into France wasn't hard. The Germans didn't know you were coming, and the bad weather meant that they really weren't watching for you too closely. But the element of surprise is gone. That means that nowhere is really safe. But you think that staying out of sight of the German fighters is still your best bet. You grip your controls as you speed away from the prison, staying almost as low as you did on the way in. You're headed west, back toward the English Channel. There's no more need to be secretive. Now, it's all about getting out of here as fast as possible.

As you pass over a small, wooded area, you spot a series of bright yellow flashes below. Suddenly, you realize that it's enemy anti-aircraft guns, hidden deep among the trees. The enemy fire rips right through the wooden hull of your plane. It blasts holes in one of the wings and knocks out a propeller.

You're lucky that you weren't injured, but your plane is badly damaged. It shudders and rattles, banking hard to one side as it descends.

"I'm hit!" you call over the radio as you struggle with your plane's controls. "One engine out. Losing altitude fast—I'm going down!"

Turn to page 28.

Your plane is too damaged to get back to safety. One of your engines is out. Your aircraft's hull and both wings have holes blasted through them. The wooden-hulled airplane isn't designed to take that kind of punishment.

Normally, you would have time to bail out. But you're flying so low to the ground, that it's not an option. You have only moments to figure out where to crash land. You quickly scan the area and spot an open field nearby.

"That will have to do," you mutter to yourself. Then you use what little control you have left to guide the plane toward the field.

The ground races toward you, and you brace yourself for impact. *THUNK!* As the plane makes a very rough landing, it skids across the snow-covered field. It only comes to a bone-rattling stop when one of its wings clips a small tree. *CRACK!*

There's no time to waste. You quickly open the cockpit and hop out. You scan the area, unsure of what to do. Maybe other allied planes will pass over this way. Should you stay in the open field to flag one down?

On the other hand, German forces will surely be looking for you as well. They could be on their way already. You could run to a nearby wooded area to hide.

To stay here and try to wave down help, turn to page 34.

To run for the woods, turn to page 36.

There's no time to think—you can only react. You abandon your original target—the barracks—and bank your plane to the right so you can switch targets.

But you're too close to the prison to make the maneuver. Instead, your hasty change of course has you pointed directly at the main three-story prison building!

You forget about your bomb and frantically pull up. The Mosquito responds quickly—but not quickly enough. One of your wings clips the building, sending your plane into a spin. Seconds later, you slam into a snowy field. With so much speed, you never have a chance. The plane erupts in a ball of fire.

You'll never know if the mission was a success. But your part in it is over.

THE END

To follow another path, turn to page 11.
To learn more about Operation Jericho, turn to page 99.

You pull up, gaining altitude. For a brief moment, all seems clear. But then you spot the German fighters coming in fast.

You quickly dive, keeping your plane on the move to evade the German fire. But the two German pilots are skilled. They are hot on your tail. You know it's only a matter of time before they get you.

Just as the German fighters close in, one of the Typhoon fighters supporting your team swoops down. The pilot opens fire, blowing the wing off one of the German fighters.

A Hawker Typhoon fighter plane

Turn the page.

As the other German fighter plane banks hard and flees, you say a silent thank-you to the Typhoon pilot. Then you head west as fast as your plane can take you. Although more German planes follow, none of them can catch you. Then bad weather sends them back when you reach the English Channel.

Soon after crossing the channel, you touch down safely at an air base in England. It feels good to finally be back on friendly soil.

Later that day, you and the other pilots attend the post-mission briefing to find out if the raid was a success. While you learn that it was considered successful, it came at a steep price. Hundreds of prisoners made it out, but many were also killed or recaptured. The Allies also lost several planes and good pilots, including Pickard, whose plane was hit shortly after the bombing.

You weigh the details in your mind. While many of the prisoners died in the explosions and the escape attempt that followed, some did manage to survive. On top of that, you completed your mission and made it back safely—which is the best you can ever hope for during this terrible war.

As the war drags on and the Allies slowly make gains, you're glad you took part in a mission to help drive the Nazis out of France.

THE END

To follow another path, turn to page 11.
To learn more about Operation Jericho, turn to page 99.

You scan the sky, desperately hoping to see an Allied airplane. After a few moments, you spot one in the distance. But it passes far from where you're standing. There's no chance they saw you. Too late, you realize that even if they did, there's nothing they could do about it. There's nowhere here they could land safely.

No help is coming, but someone is headed your way. A group of German troops has spotted you. They're rushing across the open field, weapons drawn. If you run, they'll shoot.

So, you do the only thing you can. You drop down to your knees and allow yourself to be captured.

One of the German soldiers barks something at you in German. Another pats you down and grabs you roughly by the shoulder.

Your mission was to free Allied prisoners of war. But now, you're about to become one.

THE END

To follow another path, turn to page 11.
To learn more about Operation Jericho, turn to page 99.

Even if an Allied pilot spotted you out here, there's nothing they could do to help. So, you do the only thing you can—run. You sprint as fast as you can for a nearby patch of woods. The trees are bare of leaves in winter, but they provide some cover from German forces who might be looking for you.

You wait there for perhaps an hour, huddled behind a large tree. Then you hear something—the snapping of a twig. Muffled voices. Footsteps.

You fear the worst—that the Germans have found you. But when a voice calls out, it's in French, not German. Slowly, you rise up from your hiding spot. Two young men stand before you. They're in plain clothing, not uniforms.

"Help me," you say.

The men smile. Their English is rough, but it's good enough to tell you that they are French Resistance fighters.

A group of French Resistance fighters during World War II

“Come with us,” one of them urges. They’re taking you to a safe place.

Somehow, you’re going to make it out of this alive. You know you’ve gotten incredibly lucky today.

THE END

To follow another path, turn to page 11.
To learn more about Operation Jericho, turn to page 99.

You take one last look over your shoulder. To your delight, you spot prisoners spilling out of the damaged building.

"Run, boys," you exclaim. "You can do it!"

Just then, Captain Pickard's voice crackles over the radio. "Red Daddy," he calls out.

That's the code word that means your mission is complete. Pickard is telling the third wave of planes not to attack and for everyone to get out of here.

As you follow your orders, you feel good knowing you've done your part. Now it's up to the prisoners and the French Resistance forces waiting to help them to safety.

As you fly northwest, away from Amiens, Nazi planes scramble to intercept you. You manage to get out safely, but not everyone does. Pickard's plane is hit just before it leaves. His plane crashes, and you know it's unlikely he survived.

You know that could have been you. And you can't help but think of the prisoners and all that they've been through. Your part of the mission is over. But theirs is just beginning, and many of them won't make it out alive.

You're glad to have given them a chance. But you'll always wonder if you could have done more to protect them.

THE END

To follow another path, turn to page 11.
To learn more about Operation Jericho, turn to page 99.

X100
JET PIPE °C
SLOW
FAST
KELVIN
OIL
P.S.I.

Chapter 3

BREAKING OUT

"Get up!" barks Hans, one of the guards at Amiens Prison. You wake up, startled by the sudden noise. After four months as a prisoner here, you still haven't gotten used to the rough treatment.

Hans, with his bushy mustache and sharp blue eyes, is one of your least favorite guards. Most of them treat the prisoners with some level of kindness. But Hans is a mean one.

"UP!" Hans shouts again, kicking you in the side. You're a British soldier captured by the Nazis. Some of the guards treat the British a little better. Your fellow French Resistance prisoners often get the worst of the abuse from the guards. But Hans does not seem to discriminate. He's cruel to everyone.

Turn the page.

You know better than to disobey. You're weak and terribly hungry—food is scarce and the guards give you just enough to survive.

As you stand, still half asleep, you feel faint—it's been hours since you had any water, and you're dehydrated. You almost fall back down. But you manage to keep yourself up, with your hands on your knees. Then you slowly stand up straight.

You step over the dingy mattress that serves as your bed. The room is cold and drafty. You share it with two other prisoners, Jean and Lucas. Behind you, they're slowly rising to their feet as well.

Hans leads you through the dark halls to the main doors of the prison building. Two more guards who are posted there open them. You squint as daylight floods in. It's cloudy, but you've been inside so long that it seems blindingly bright.

The daylight reflects off the fresh blanket of snow that covers everything. A few flakes are still falling. If you could ignore the fact that you're in a prison, it would almost be pretty.

"Outside," Hans orders, giving you a rough shove in the back.

You move quickly, knowing that Hans will whack you with his baton if you don't obey right away. And you're eager to go.

The entrance to Amiens Prison surrounded by tall brick walls and a memorial dedicated to those who died during Operation Jericho

Turn the page.

Time outside is a rarity. It's cold and damp, but seeing the sky over your head warms your heart. Sometimes it's hard to remember that there's a whole world beyond the prison walls.

You, Jean, Lucas, and about a dozen other prisoners spend a few hours outside. Some of the prisoners walk around the grounds, under the close watch of the guards. But you're so weak and hungry that you mostly just sit. You talk a little, but too much chatter draws the attention of the guards. So, you just enjoy the cool fresh air.

Just as Hans comes to order you back inside, you hear a strange sound. It's a low buzzing sound. Suddenly, the guards begin shouting in German. In the time you've been held captive in Amiens, you've picked up enough German to understand what they're saying.

Das Flugzeug. It means airplane.

You look to the sky, but all you see are heavy gray clouds.

"Where is it?" Jean asks. All three of you scan the sky, eager to spot the plane with hopes it belongs to the Allies.

The buzzing sound grows louder. It's not just one plane, you realize. It's several.

"Inside!" Hans shouts, shoving you roughly through the door. It slams behind you. Inside, the guards are shouting, rushing past you.

Suddenly, the ground shakes as a huge explosion rocks the outer walls. Then another blast rattles the ground . . . and then another.

"It's an air raid!" Lucas shouts. "The Allies are busting us out! Everyone, get down!"

You drop down and cover your head with your hands. Moments later, an explosion rocks the building. Then another.

Turn the page.

The power of the blast blows the doors open. You can feel the heat from the explosion on your skin. Debris rains down all around you. Something heavy slams into your shoulder.

Then, after a couple of short minutes, it's over. A pile of stone and debris lies in front of the open doors. You can hear guards shouting outside. Then you hear the pop of gunfire.

Lucas grabs you by the arm. "Get up!" he shouts. "This is our chance!"

Jean interrupts him. "The guards are out there," he says. "Don't you hear them shooting? We should wait here . . . at least for a little bit."

Lucas shakes his head, then looks at you. "I'm going. The longer we wait, the more time the guards will have to react and organize. Come with me if you want."

To go with Lucas, go to page 47.

To stay here with Jean, turn to page 49.

Lucas is right. If this is an Allied air raid to break you out of prison, you can't hesitate. You've got to go. You climb over the pile of rubble and return outside. As you scan your surroundings, you see that everything is chaos.

Allied bombers conducting an air raid on Amiens Prison

Turn the page.

Guards are firing their guns at the sky. To the south and west, small, low-flying airplanes are quickly disappearing over the horizon.

In the chaos, you see that the Allied bombs have blasted holes in the north and east outer walls, as well as several holes in the main prison building. Already, your fellow prisoners are pouring outside.

"Over there," Lucas says, pointing to the destroyed east wall. "We can get out."

It's the closest way out of here, but you count at least four guards between you and the wall. The north wall is farther away, but you only see one guard in that direction. Which way should you go?

To go to the nearby east wall, turn to page 52.

To head for the north wall farther away, turn to page 54.

You're in no shape to make a run for it. You decide to stick with Jean.

"Good luck, Lucas," you call out. Then you watch your friend scramble over the rubble and run across the open field outside.

And that's when you realize Lucas is not alone. Others are streaming out as well. It's chaos outside. The guards are shooting, but the number of prisoners trying to escape grows by the second. Not all of them are going to make it—but you're starting to believe some of them are bound to escape.

"Look, Jean!" you shout as you point toward Lucas and the other fleeing prisoners. "If they can make it out, maybe we can as well!"

"No," Jean replies. "It's not safe out there." He grabs you by the arm. "Come on, let's wait this out in our cell. That should be about the safest place for us."

Turn the page.

Just then, a group of four prisoners brushes past you. They're headed straight for the hole in the wall.

"What are you two doing?" one of the prisoners asks as they hurry past. "This is your chance! You have to go, now. Don't just stand there!"

Outside, the shouting and gunfire makes it sound like a true battle is underway. Dust still hangs in the air from the explosions. The guards may be shooting, but they're almost as confused and disoriented as you are. If you were ever going to make a run for it, there would be no better time than now.

You reach for Jean, but he flinches and takes a step in the opposite direction.

"I already told you," Jean says. "I'm staying right here." Then he takes another step deeper into the building.

You take a long look at him. He's so thin. His face is dirty and his hair is a mess. There's no spark in his eyes.

You realize that life in a prison camp has broken him. He doesn't have the will to escape. But you know that looking at Jean could be like looking in a mirror. If you stay, how much longer can you survive? Can you make it until the end of the war? Do you even want to?

To follow the men outside, turn to page 56.

To return to your cell with Jean, turn to page 64.

Lucas is already a long way ahead of you, bolting for the hole in the east wall. You're too weak to run, but you move as quickly as you can.

"Stop!" you hear one of the guards shout. Lucas, only a few dozen steps from the prison's damaged outer wall, doesn't slow down a bit. He's almost through the opening when the guard opens fire. You watch in horror as your friend crumples to the ground.

Amiens Prison's roof damaged by Allied bombers

You drop to all fours and cover your head. You hope the guards won't notice you in the chaos. It works. A stream of prisoners is pouring out of the building now, and the guards turn their attention to them.

You don't waste the opportunity. With every bit of strength you have, you pick yourself up off of the cold ground and rush to the wall. As you climb over the rubble from the blast and step outside the prison walls, you're almost overcome with joy. But you know that you're not safe yet.

Turn to page 58.

For a moment, the guards were shocked by the sudden air raid. But that brief time of surprise has passed. They understand what's happening now, and they're shooting prisoners who are trying to escape. You want to stay as far from them as possible, so you head toward the north wall.

You try to run, but in your weakened condition you can barely manage a brisk walk. It's a long way to go. Ahead of you, other prisoners are rushing through the blasted wall. But the pop-pop-pop of gunfire rattles through the courtyard.

With the haze of dust, the ringing of gunfire, and the sounds of shouting and screaming, you suddenly feel dizzy. The world around you seems like a dream. Nothing seems real.

Pull yourself together, man! you think. *You've got to keep moving!*

"Halt!" a deep, booming voice suddenly shouts from behind. In your confusion, you're not even sure that the guard is yelling at you.

If you ignore the order and keep going, you might finally be free. But if the guard is addressing you, maybe it would be better to stop and get down on the ground.

To ignore the order and keep going, turn to page 60.

To stop and get down on the ground, turn to page 62.

"I'm sorry, Jean," you say. "I have to try to escape."

Jean just nods slowly. "Good luck, my friend," he says. "I hope we meet again."

With that, you follow the men through the hole in the wall. As you step outside, an airplane streaks across the sky. The pilot opens fire on the guard barracks—where many of the guards are still gathered. Some of the prisoners let out a cheer as the plane climbs and then speeds out of sight.

With that, the skies are empty—the Allied planes have done their part. You hope all the brave pilots make it back okay. Now it's time for you to do your part.

You don't have the strength, but you head as quickly as you can for the hole blasted in the east wall. While the guards are trying to stop the stream of escaping prisoners, there aren't enough of them to stop everyone.

When you make it to the breach in the wall, you scramble over the broken pile of rubble. Bullets zip through the air and ping off of the rubble all around you. You stumble as you climb over the collapsed section of outer wall, but another prisoner quickly grabs your arm and helps you up.

As you finally step down onto the snow-covered ground, you realize that you're outside of Amiens Prison for the first time in months. It feels amazing. But what do you do now?

Turn to page 58.

Outside of the prison walls, escaping prisoners stream in several directions. You scan the terrain, looking for some sort of cover. There's not much. The land immediately around the prison is mostly open, snow-covered fields. A road runs along one side of the prison, but you know to avoid that. It's sure to be crawling with Germans. In the other direction, a mile or two away, you see a wooded area. It's exactly the sort of cover you need to hide.

You head in that direction. It's a slow, exhausting walk through the snow. Your feet are wet and your legs ache from the effort. It's been months since you had proper exercise and your strength fades quickly. You half expect to be stopped by German forces at any moment. But that doesn't happen. You continue on, and after what feels like hours, you reach the woods.

You slump down onto the ground next to a tree, gasping for breath. What next? Where will you go? You have to find somewhere safe. You'll freeze if you stay out here long.

As you catch your breath, you hear footsteps and several men's voices. It sounds like they're speaking French, but you can't be sure. Panic rises up in you. Could it be Germans searching for escaped prisoners? Or could it be friendly forces, here to rescue you as part of the raid?

To call out to the men, turn to page 66.

To hide from them, turn to page 69.

You shake your head, trying to clear the cobwebs in your mind. It's just enough to give you a little bit of clarity. The north wall is still a few hundred feet ahead of you. If you have any hope of getting out of this terrible prison, you have to keep going.

You take a few steps forward.

"HALT!" shouts the voice again. This time, there's no doubt. The guard is talking to you.

The air raid's bombs hit the prison's buildings and walls and destroyed the guards' barracks.

You clench your jaw and keep going. You won't lie down and spend another day in this prison. You take two steps . . . then two more. You know what is going to happen, but you refuse to turn around.

The shot rings out. The guards are shooting anyone they see trying to escape. So many prisoners are rushing for the walls, they can't shoot them all. Many will get out alive.

Sadly, you won't be one of them.

THE END

To follow another path, turn to page 11.
To learn more about Operation Jericho, turn to page 99.

The wall is still so far away. You're not sure you could even make it that far if nobody was shooting at you. So, you do the only thing you can. You drop down to your knees, then lay down flat on the cold ground.

From that moment on, everything happens in a haze. One of the guards grabs you and roughly leads you back inside a part of the prison that hasn't been blasted open.

"Thought you could get away, huh?" the guard growls in German. "Well, think again. It's back in a cell for you."

The guard shoves you into a cell with several dozen other prisoners. As the door clangs shut, you notice that many of these prisoners are hurt—some by the explosions from the raid, others by gunshots. Their cries of pain are too much to bear and you slump down to the ground. All you want to do is close your eyes.

Your hopes to escape have been dashed. You're still a prisoner of war. All you can do now is hope you survive prison long enough for this terrible war to end. That's probably your only chance to get back home.

THE END

To follow another path, turn to page 11.
To learn more about Operation Jericho, turn to page 99.

Your shoulders slump as you make your decision to stay. The prison hasn't just broken Jean. It's broken you as well. You don't have the will to try an escape.

Together, you move slowly through the hallways. Other prisoners rush past you in their hurry to attempt escape. Their faces are bright and alive. They understand the danger. But they're willing to risk it all for their freedom. You envy them as you arrive back at your empty cell.

With a sigh, you slip back into your cell and collapse onto your uncomfortable mattress. In here, you can barely hear the chaos outside. You close your eyes. All you want to do is sleep.

You'll remain a prisoner, but this time it's by your own choice. Maybe you can manage to stay alive until the war is over. But at the moment, that feels unlikely.

THE END

To follow another path, turn to page 11.
To learn more about Operation Jericho, turn to page 99.

You can't know who is out there. But one thing is sure. You have no chance of getting out alive without help.

"I'm here," you shout. Your voice is weak and scratchy. You call out again. "Someone help me! Please!"

The crunching sound of footsteps in the snow grows louder as they head your way. Moments later, three figures appear through the trees.

Relief washes over you as you realize that these are not German troops. They're French Resistance fighters!

"Come with us," says one of the men as they help you to your feet. "But do not speak. We're not out of danger just yet."

They lead you through the woods. It's a winding route that eventually takes you to a small farmhouse on the other side. A feeling of relief washes over you as you step inside.

The men set you down in a soft chair in front of a crackling fire. Your shoulders slump, and you finally relax a little.

"You were lucky we found you," says one of the men. "The Germans were shooting escaped prisoners on sight. We've rescued hundreds. But there are many more we couldn't help."

"What will happen to me now?" you ask. "Will you be able to keep me hidden? Can you get me back home to England?"

Turn the page.

The man nods. “Don’t worry. We’ll take care of everything. You rest now. Soon, we’ll have you back home.”

You close your eyes, thinking about Jean and Lucas. Will you ever see either of them again? You hope so. For now, you’re just grateful to be out of the awful Amiens Prison.

THE END

To follow another path, turn to page 11.
To learn more about Operation Jericho, turn to page 99.

You are paralyzed by fear. The idea of calling out to the men fills you with terror. If they're Germans, they'll shoot you on sight. After all you've gone through, you just don't want to take that risk.

You realize your best option is to find a better place to hide. You scan the woods around you and spot a large fallen tree nearby. As quickly as you can, you scramble over and crawl behind it.

Turn the page.

As you lie behind the fallen tree, you listen carefully. Sure enough, the sound of the footsteps gets louder—and then they stop. Most unsettling, you don't hear any voices at all now.

Are they listening for me? you wonder.

You lie perfectly still and try to keep your breathing as silent as possible. After a few minutes, the footsteps start up again and gradually fade as the men walk away.

You breathe a sigh of relief. Whoever that was never saw you.

Hours pass. You're freezing. You can't feel your feet. You don't feel like it's safe to leave the woods, but you have to find somewhere to go. Maybe you could find an abandoned barn to sleep in.

You stumble back out into the open field. You trudge through the snow, but you're moving so slowly.

Unfortunately, German troops are still out combing the countryside, looking for escaped prisoners. When they spot you, you never have a chance. You can barely move. They approach with their weapons raised. You can tell right away that they do not intend to capture you again. They're going to shoot you.

You close your eyes and imagine home. You hoped you could see it again someday. But your story ends here.

THE END

To follow another path, turn to page 11.
To learn more about Operation Jericho, turn to page 99.

X100
JET PIPE °C
20
10
30
OIL
P.S.I.
0
40
SLOW
FAST
TYPE KB 301/02
KELVIN

Chapter 4

THE FRENCH RESISTANCE

You are a French citizen living in northern France. As you walk down the streets of your hometown, you can almost forget that your country is at the center of World War II in Europe. Light snow covers the ground. Warm light glows in the windows of many of the houses you pass. It's evening, and all is quiet. It seems very far from the battles that rage on in other parts of France and beyond.

Then you round a corner and get a cold reminder. A Nazi flag hangs from the largest house in town. The German forces that have taken over France have seized the house. It serves as a center of operations in their ongoing war.

Turn the page.

You grit your teeth. The occupying Nazi forces expect the French people to be passive. They want you to be easily ruled. But that's not who you are.

You turn down a dark alley and duck into the back storeroom of a local shop. A single light bulb casts a dim light on the small room. Half a dozen other people are huddled inside, talking in hushed tones. Several of them nod to you.

You are all French Resistance fighters. You fight against the Nazi occupation in secret, doing anything you can to make life difficult for the enemy. One of your group's leaders, a young woman named Marie, is telling the group about the latest news in the Resistance.

"The Allies are planning an air raid on Amiens Prison," she explains. That makes everyone's ears perk up.

You are very familiar with Amiens Prison—it's only a few dozen miles from here, and it's where many captured Resistance fighters end up. If the Allies could free those prisoners, it would make a huge difference in the Resistance movement.

Marie points to the storeroom's rear wall, where two German SS uniforms hang. "We've managed to get a hold of these uniforms. We need two people to use them to gather intelligence about the prison, its defenses, and its weaknesses. It will be a dangerous mission, but it's critical to its success."

"What about the rest of us?" asks Henri, an older man who only recently joined the Resistance.

Marie nods. "We don't know exactly when the raid will take place. It's likely that the Allies don't know yet either—it will depend on the weather. But once it happens, they're

Turn the page.

counting on us to help the escaped prisoners. We'll need to get them to safety right away. That means we need to know when the raid is coming. I want to post lookouts near the prison who can send word as soon as the raid begins."

You think about both parts of the mission. You speak a little German, so maybe you'd be well suited to serve as one of the spies. On the other hand, serving as a lookout is probably a lot safer. What should you do?

To serve as a spy, go to page 77.

To offer to be a lookout, turn to page 81.

The German uniform doesn't fit you well. It's tight across the chest and the pants are half an inch too short for you.

"Are you sure this is going to work?" you ask Marie.

"It's not a great fit," Marie admits. "But it will have to do."

You, Marie, and another Resistance fighter, Maurice, travel together to Amiens. The two of them will try to gather information about the prison's walls. They'll pretend to be a German officer walking with his girlfriend near the prison's perimeter.

Your job is much harder. You have to go inside, disguised as a courier. You'll pretend to be delivering a package to the prison warden's office. But really you'll be collecting detailed information for the Allies about the layout of the prison and the daily routines of the guards and prisoners.

Turn the page.

Your heart races as you approach the checkpoint to get in. Even though it is cold outside, you feel tiny beads of sweat form across your brow.

When the guard at the checkpoint sees your uniform, he quickly snaps to attention. Trying to act confident, you hand him a permit that the Resistance somehow managed to obtain. You hope he doesn't notice your hand trembling as you hand it over.

The guard glances over the permit. You hold your breath in nervous anticipation. But then, almost to your surprise, he reaches over and opens the gate.

"Report to the warden's office," he tells you in German.

You nod slightly and briskly walk past him. As you enter, you breathe a quiet sigh of relief and scan the prison grounds. The large stone building is lined with windows.

You note every detail in your mind—the location of the doors, the guard's barracks, the spacing between the walls and the buildings. You walk slowly across the field, trying to take in where guards are stationed, searching for watchtowers, weapon placements, and more. Every detail you can report will help the Allies plan the raid.

As you approach the large building, another guard stops you.

"Show me your papers," he barks out. Once again, you hand over your permit.

This guard looks much more carefully at the documents.

"Why is this permit so old?" he asks you.

You speak German fairly well, but you know that if you say too much, your accent could give you away. So you shrug.

"It's all I have," you reply.

Turn the page.

The man looks at you with deep suspicion in his eyes. "One moment," he finally says. "I need to show this permit to my superior."

You're afraid he's not buying your act. Should you wait for the guard to return or abort the mission now?

To wait for the guard to return, turn to page 83.

To turn and march back to the gate, turn to page 90.

You're not sure you can successfully pull off impersonating a German officer. So, you offer to serve as a lookout instead.

The next day, you travel to the town of Amiens. Your job is to watch the prison and keep an eye open for signs of the raid.

The prison is surrounded mainly by open fields. A few miles away, a wooded area provides some cover. You have binoculars, a radio, and basic supplies.

French binoculars used during World War II

Turn the page.

You and a few others will take turns watching the prison and reporting back anything you see. A small farmhouse nearby will serve as a base, where you'll sleep and eat meals.

Over the next week, you fall into a daily routine. You spend hours watching the prison from afar. You note some nearby troop movements, as well as the arrival of new prisoners. But there's no sign of the raid.

Then one day, something unusual happens. You hear the sound of gunfire from inside the prison. You try to see what's happening through your binoculars, but whatever is happening is taking place on the opposite side of the building. You can't see a thing.

To stay here and keep watching, turn to page 85.

To leave the woods and get a closer look, turn to page 92.

You take a deep breath. Trying to leave now would look more suspicious. You have to appear calm and confident. After a few moments, the guard returns.

"I'm sorry, sir," he says. "My supervisor tells me that some offices are still using the older permits. You can go ahead."

You simply nod and slowly walk inside.

As you move down the hallway, you take careful mental notes about everything you see. The layout of the building, the guard postings, the locations of stairwells.

You reach the warden's office and drop off the small package you've been carrying. You don't even know what's inside—probably some faked documents. It doesn't matter because it's all part of your ruse to get a look at the inner workings of the prison. You turn back the way you came. Within minutes, you're back outside the prison walls.

Turn the page.

That night, you sit down and sketch everything you saw. Another member of the Resistance will get the information to the Allied forces planning the air raid. You feel confident that your report will help make a difference.

The following days are long. You know that the raid is coming, but you don't know exactly when. On the morning of February 18, heavy clouds and snow settle in over the area. The Allies use the bad weather as an opportunity. Late that morning, you get the word—the raid is on! You rush out to the prison, where the action is already underway. Allied bombers have blasted holes in the prison walls and main building. Already, men are streaming out of the prison. They need your help!

Turn to page 88.

You can't risk getting any closer. If German guards spot you, they'll either capture you or they'll just shoot you on sight. Besides, your main job here is to watch for the raid. The Resistance forces have to be ready as soon as it begins. If all goes according to plan, there will be a lot of prisoners escaping, and you've got to get them to safety.

So, you stay put, watching and waiting, silent and patient. After a few minutes, the shooting stops. Once again, all is quiet.

The next morning, you're back at your post. It's a cold, wet day. Heavy clouds fill the sky, and snowflakes leave a fresh, white blanket on the land. Your mind begins to wander as you sit, just waiting for something to happen. Part of you begins to doubt that the raid is ever coming. Did the Allies change their mind?

Turn the page.

That's when you hear it—a low buzzing sound, coming from the northeast. It's an airplane! No . . . it's a bunch of airplanes! You grab your radio and frantically warn your fellow Resistance fighters.

"The raid is starting," you say. "Allied bombers are coming in very low. Get everyone out here, it's time!"

You watch in awe as the small bomber planes speed overhead. They're flying so low that it looks like they're going to land. But they don't. They dive toward the prison dropping bombs. One after the other, the bombs skip off of the ground and slam into the heavy stone walls of the prison.

BOOM! A huge section of the prison wall blasts open.

BOOM! Another bomb creates a second opening in the prison wall.

Moments later, more planes come swooping in. Instead of targeting the prison wall, they bomb the large three-story prison building itself, as well as the small guards' barracks attached to each end of it.

Within minutes, prisoners are streaming out of the prison. They need your help.

Prisoners fleeing from Amiens Prison

Turn the page.

As prisoners pour out of the prison walls, many of them scatter. They don't know where to go. The guards continue shooting from the prison, but they're overwhelmed.

Meanwhile, your fellow Resistance fighter, Henri, approaches from behind. He stops beside you to watch some of the escaped prisoners heading in your direction.

"What should we do?" you ask.

"The Nazis will organize quickly," he says. "We have to get as many of these people out of here as we can before that happens."

Henri rushes to the side of the first young man who approaches. He takes the man by the arm and leads him in the direction of the safe house you've been using.

Moments later, a group of four men trudge through the snow on your left. They're headed in the opposite direction of town. There's nowhere for them to go in that direction.

At the same time, you spot a much larger group meandering through the snow on your right. This group looks shocked and confused, and one of the men is bleeding badly from a wound on his head. He needs medical attention soon.

Both groups clearly need your help, but you can't go to them both at the same time. Which group should you help?

To help the small group of men, turn to page 94.

To go to the larger group, turn to page 96.

You start to panic. You're certain the guard suspects you. His superior officer is sure to question you about the permit, and your accent is almost guaranteed to give you away.

You turn on your heel and march back toward the gate. You're in such a rush to get out of here that you're almost running.

Unfortunately, your sudden and erratic behavior gets you instant attention. Two more guards move in front of the gate to block your path. Then, from behind, the first guard returns with your permit.

"Stop that man!" the guard with your permit shouts. "He's a spy!"

You try to dodge, but there is nowhere to go. The gate guards grab you by the arms. They search you for weapons and drag you back inside the building. The prison warden waits inside. He gives you a grin as you stand before him.

"Well, well," he says, smirking. "We used to have to go out and find members of the French Resistance. Now, it seems they've started marching right into the prison for us."

You've failed your mission. Instead of helping with the escape, you'll now be one of the prisoners struggling to make it out alive.

THE END

To follow another path, turn to page 11.
To learn more about Operation Jericho, turn to page 99.

You really want to know what's happening. It could be important. Are they shooting prisoners? If so, the Allies will want to know. Information like that might force them to carry out the raid sooner.

For the first time, you venture outside of the forest. It feels very strange to leave the cover of the trees. You move carefully across the open field, trying to position yourself for a better view. When you're less than a mile from the prison, you look through your binoculars again.

"Dang, I still can't see anything," you mutter to yourself. "Do I dare go any closer to the prison?"

Before you can even answer your own question, a prison guard spots you. From his wild gestures to a second guard, it's clear he thinks someone spying on the prison with binoculars is a threat.

Not wasting a moment, you turn and run as the guards raise their rifles.

But you're too late. You're well within their range. Shots ring out across the open countryside. The first two miss you. The third slams into the snow just a few inches from your feet.

The fourth shot doesn't miss. You got reckless, and you'll pay for that with your life.

THE END

To follow another path, turn to page 11.
To learn more about Operation Jericho, turn to page 99.

Those four men are running the wrong way. You have to tell them.

"Stop!" you shout. "There's nothing that way!"

You take off running after the men. One of them looks over his shoulder and sees you coming. That's when you realize they don't know who you are. They're not running toward something. They're running away from you!

You keep following them. The men are weak and underfed. You are much stronger and faster. Soon, you catch up to the men.

"Please, stop! I'm here to help!" you insist.

Finally, the men stop. They are doubled over, trying to catch their breath. They've spent every bit of energy they have.

On the horizon, German forces from the city are closing in.

"We have to go, now!" you say. The men do their best, but they are too slow. The Germans catch up long before you can get the men to safety.

"Well, well," says one of the German officers as he raises his gun. "We can't have prisoners escaping." He looks at you. His blue eyes are cold, seeming to stare right through you. "And after today, we're not in the mood for taking prisoners."

You close your eyes, knowing that your story ends here.

THE END

To follow another path, turn to page 11.
To learn more about Operation Jericho, turn to page 99.

You hurry over to the large group. About 15 men are gathered. Two of them help the injured man, supporting him on either side.

"Everyone, with me," you call out. Most of these prisoners are French Resistance fighters themselves, so they immediately realize what you're doing.

You lead the group across the open field. "The Germans will be out in force. We have to go fast," you insist.

The men give every ounce of energy they have. They're starving and exhausted, but they push themselves harder than you ever imagined they could.

Their effort pays off. You manage to lead the whole group to the isolated farmhouse.

"Everyone inside," you say. You want these men out of sight as soon as possible. "We have food and water. Get in quickly, please."

As the last man files in, you scan the horizon. No sign of the Germans.

You let out a deep breath. You did it. Now it's time to do more. Others inside will take care of these men. You're going back out to see if you can find anyone else.

THE END

To follow another path, turn to page 11.
To learn more about Operation Jericho, turn to page 99.

X100
JET PIPE °C
OIL
P.S.I.
SLOW
FAST
TYPE KB 501/02
KELVIN

Chapter 5

WORLD WAR II AND OPERATION JERICHO

World War II was a brutal, bloody war. It began in 1939 when Germany, controlled by the Nazi Party, invaded Poland. Other nations including Italy and Japan soon joined Germany in the fight. Together, they were called the Axis powers. Meanwhile, the Allied nations formed to stop the Axis powers. The Allies included the United States, the Soviet Union, Great Britain, France, Australia, and others.

An estimated 15 million soldiers died in combat, with another 25 million wounded. Even worse, the war took the lives of tens of millions of civilians.

Meanwhile, hundreds of thousands of Allied soldiers were captured and sent to prison camps during the war. Life was hard for prisoners of war (POWs). The conditions were poor. There was little food—sometimes none at all. Some POWs were denied clean drinking water. Disease ran rampant through many camps, and there was no real medical care for sick prisoners. POWs sometimes faced mental and physical abuse. Some prisoners had to perform hard labor. Others had nothing to do, and boredom contributed to depression. Many prisoners did not survive the harsh conditions.

Prison escapes were rare, but they did happen. Prisons were usually isolated and well-guarded. But sometimes, prisoners outsmarted their guards. In one of the most famous escapes, prisoners held in the German prison Stalag Luft III dug a tunnel under the prison walls and crawled out.

Captured Royal Air Force officers at Stalag Luft III lay the foundation for a new barracks that they would later use for starting an underground tunnel.

In another prison, a group secretly built a ladder and climbed over a barbed-wire fence. One prisoner even made a fake German uniform and simply walked out of prison!

Amiens Prison was located just outside the town of Amiens in northern France. The large three-story building was surrounded by an imposing stone wall, making any hope of escape almost impossible.

Amiens Prison held more than 700 Allied POWs in early 1944. They included both soldiers and officers. But many of the Allied prisoners were members of the French Resistance—citizens who were secretly fighting the German occupation of France. The French Resistance provided the Allies with critical military intelligence, including German troop movements within France. In 1944, Allied commanders hatched a plan to bomb the prison walls to give the prisoners a chance to escape.

The mission, code-named Operation Jericho, launched on February 18, 1944. A group of Mosquito bombers and Typhoon fighters took off from England. They flew through a snowstorm over the English Channel and into France. Flying low over the ground to avoid detection, three waves of bombers were set to attack.

Damage to Amiens Prison during Operation Jericho

The first wave blasted holes in the outer walls. The second bombed the prison building itself. The third wave never attacked—they weren't needed. Within minutes of the second wave's attack, prisoners could be seen streaming out of the prison. The aircraft quickly headed back to England. During the raid, two planes and their crews were lost. One of the men who died in the raid was Captain Charles Pickard, the commanding officer of the mission.

Meanwhile, German guards responded quickly and brutally to escaping prisoners. They opened fire, shooting prisoners at will. Many prisoners still made it out. French Resistance fighters waited beyond the prison walls to help guide them to safety. In total, 258 POWs made it out. However, many of them were recaptured shortly after the raid.

The raid was a success in some ways. It did free some POWs, including important members of the French Resistance. But it was a failure in many ways as well. More than 100 POWs were killed in the explosions, and many more died at the hands of the Germans in the hours and days that followed. In addition, two planes were lost, along with their crew. Because more prisoners died than were rescued, many people questioned whether such a risky raid was worth it.

Freed British POWs arrive back in England in May 1945.

World War II ended in 1945. Germany surrendered on May 7. Japan followed on August 14, after U.S. bombers dropped atomic bombs on the cities of Hiroshima and Nagasaki. After the war, most surviving POWs were released. Their long ordeal was over.

MORE ABOUT OPERATION JERICHO

››› One of the Mosquito bomber pilots carried a small movie camera. The pilot filmed the raid. The film shows the Mosquitoes soaring across the English Channel and later approaching the prison for their bombing pass. The film of the raid was a rarity at the time and helped make Operation Jericho famous.

››› The details about how the French Resistance gathered information about Amiens Prison are sketchy. But historians believe one French Resistance fighter may have entered the prison disguised as a courier. He used his trip to make detailed sketches of the prison, tracking the guards and their movements. His sketches, combined with stolen blueprints of the prison's layout, helped the Allied forces plan their attack. Meanwhile, another Resistance fighter tried to learn the thickness of the prison's outer walls. He pretended to be on a walk with his girlfriend near the prison while he was noting details about the wall.

››› Two waves of bombers hit Amiens Prison. A third wave was ready to strike. But the raid's commanding officer, Captain Charles Pickard, called them off. The first two waves had done the job. Several Mosquitoes came back around to fire at the guards' barracks, then they headed back toward England.

››› Captain Pickard was the commanding officer of the raid. Earlier in his career, Pickard had taken part in an English film, *Target for To-night*. The film made him a minor celebrity in England. Pickard's plane was hit by enemy fire shortly after the bombing. He died when the plane crashed.

››› In the years that followed, Operation Jericho became a source of controversy. The raid killed more prisoners than it freed. And some French Resistance leaders deny that they ever even asked for it. However, several important Resistance leaders were saved, and they were able to provide important information about high-ranking German agents.

››› Amiens Prison still stands more than 80 years after the raid. Visitors can see the buildings that were at the center of the rescue. A plaque there honors the men who died in the raid.

THE DH.98 MOSQUITO

Nicknamed "The Wooden Wonder," the DH.98 Mosquito was one of the fastest planes in the Royal Air Force. Its wooden build and lack of on-board weapons made the plane light, maneuverable, and lightning-fast.

Workers lift a wooden part of a DH.98 Mosquito bomber at a factory in England.

TIMELINE

SEPTEMBER 1, 1939—World War II officially begins after German forces invade Poland.

MAY 10, 1940—Germany invades France. The Battle of France lasts a little more than a month before the Germans prevail.

NOVEMBER 15, 1941—The Royal Air Force takes its first delivery of the DH.98 Mosquito. More than 7,000 of the planes are built over the next decade.

DECEMBER 7, 1941—Japanese planes bomb Pearl Harbor, Hawaii. The next day, the United States enters the war to fight with the Allied forces.

OCTOBER 1943—German forces occupying France crack down on the French Resistance fighters. Many are arrested, and some are sent to Amiens Prison in northern France.

FEBRUARY 18, 1944—Operation Jericho takes place. Allied forces strike Amiens Prison at around noon, blasting holes in the prison walls to allow prisoners to escape.

FEBRUARY 21, 1944—Two Mosquitoes and four Typhoons return to Amiens to take photographs of the prison. One of the Typhoon pilots is killed after his plane is hit by enemy fire.

JUNE 6, 1944—The Allies launch a massive attack on German forces in France. The Allied invasion, called D-Day, marked a major turning point in the war and helped force Germany out of France.

AUGUST 31, 1944—Allied troops drive German forces out of Amiens, liberating the city.

MAY 7, 1945—Germany surrenders, ending the war in Europe.

AUGUST 1945—U.S. bomber planes drop atomic bombs on the Japanese cities of Hiroshima and Nagasaki. Japan surrenders a few days later.

GLOSSARY

altitude (AL-ti-tood)—the height of something above sea level or Earth's surface

barracks (BAR-uhks)—a building where soldiers are housed

citizen (SI-tuh-zuhn)—a member of a country or state who has the right to live there

cockpit (KOK-pit)—the place where a pilot sits in an airplane

execute (EK-suh-kyoot)—to kill someone as a punishment for a crime

impersonate (im-PUR-suh-nate)—to pretend to be someone else

intelligence (in-TEL-uh-jenss)—military information about an enemy force

occupy (OK-yuh-pye)—to take possession or control of an area, such as a country, by military invasion

payload (PAY-lohd)—weapons or cargo carried by an airplane

radar (RAY-dar)—an electronic device that uses radio waves to determine the location of an object such as a flying airplane

raid (RAYD)—a sudden, unexpected attack

Soviet Union (SOH-vee-et YOON-yuhn)—a former federation of 15 republics that included Russia, Ukraine, and other nations of eastern Europe and northern Asia

suspicion (suh-SPISH-uhn)—a thought, based more on feeling than on fact, that something is wrong or bad

READ MORE

Doeden, Matt. *Can You Survive a World War II Escape?: An Interactive History Adventure.* North Mankato, MN: Capstone Press, 2024.

Havemeyer, Janie. *World War II in Europe.* Minneapolis: Core Library, 2025.

Monroe, Alex. *World War II.* Minneapolis: Bellwether Media, Inc., 2024.

INTERNET SITES

Ducksters: World War II
ducksters.com/history/world_war_ii

History for Kids: World War II
historyforkids.net/world-war-two.html

National World War II Museum
www.nationalww2museum.org/learn/education/for-students

ABOUT THE AUTHOR

Matt Doeden is a freelance author and editor from Minnesota. He's written numerous children's books on sports, music, current events, the military, extreme survival, and much more. His book *It's Outta Here* was included on Bank Street's Best Books of the Year List in 2022. He lives in Minnesota with his wife and two children.

MORE BOOKS IN THIS SERIES

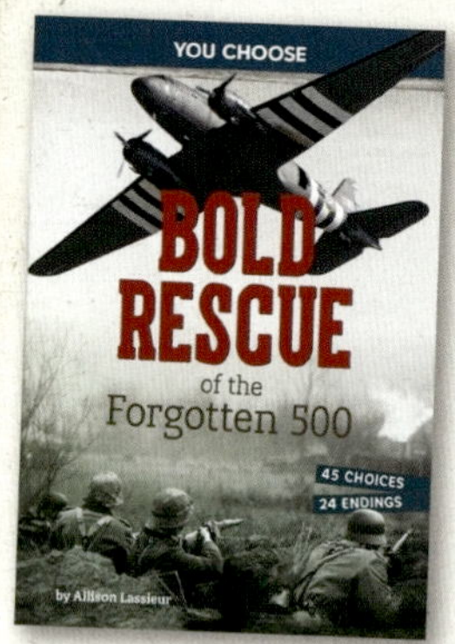

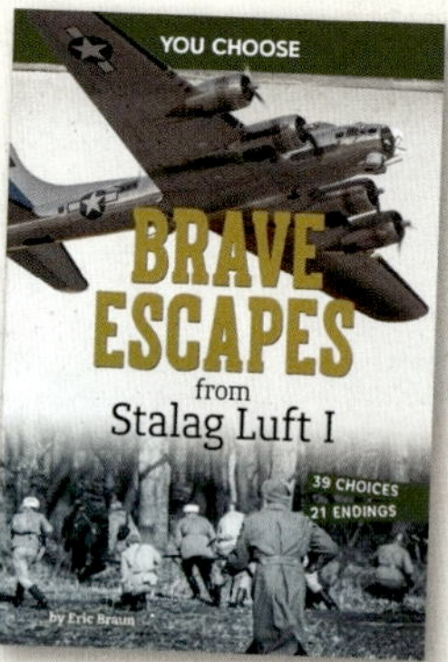

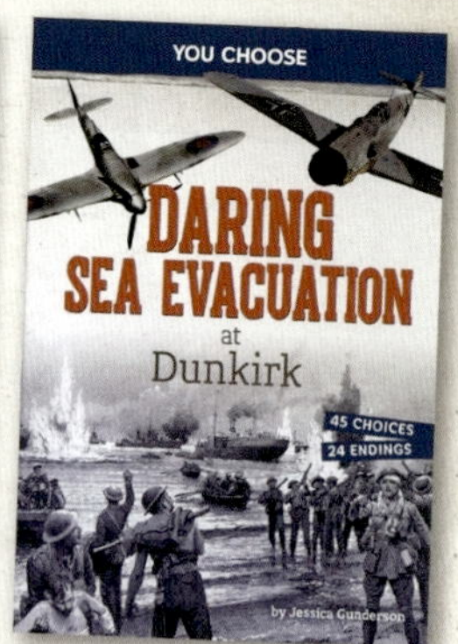